ISTHISANOLOGY?

ISTHISANOLOGY?

Written by
Amanda Bulman & **Ruth Lawrence**

Illustrated by **Leon Chung**

BREAKWATER
P.O. Box 2188, St. John's, NL, Canada, A1C 6E6
www.breakwaterbooks.com

COPYRIGHT © 2023 Amanda Bulman & Ruth Lawrence
ILLUSTRATIONS © 2023 Leon Chung
ISBN 978-1-55081-969-4

A CIP catalogue record for this book is available from Library and Archives Canada.

We acknowledge the support of the Canada Council for the Arts.
We acknowledge the financial support of the Government of Canada and the Government of Newfoundland and Labrador through the Department of Tourism, Culture, Arts and Recreation for our publishing activities.

PRINTED AND BOUND IN CANADA.

Breakwater Books is committed to choosing papers and materials for our books that help to protect our environment. To this end, this book is printed on a recycled paper and other controlled sources that are certified by the Forest Stewardship Council®.

 Conseil des arts du Canada Canada Council for the Arts

 Canadä

Newfoundland Labrador

DEDICATION

Amanda Bulman: To my nieces, Olivia, Abby, Cecily, and Paisley-Jane. I hope you'll always find joy in nature. And to my favourite two-year-old, Frank, who gets into everything and keeps his fantastic mom and dad busy.

Ruth Lawrence: To Luke and all the wonderful children and godchildren in my life—of all ages— who share the love of books.

CONTENTS

SCIENCE IS AMAZING, HUH? THERE'S SO MUCH TO KNOW, LEARN, AND DISCOVER.

Getting started can be challenging. Sometimes, just diving in is best when you're learning something new! Other times, talking to an expert is a good starting point. I call scientific experts ologists. Some of the experts in this book went to school for a long time, but other ologists learned through hands-on experience. This book will look at the ologies (fields of study) that excite me the most. We'll talk to some experts and get involved by experimenting and by examining the world around us!

I chose to look at the study of birds (ornithology), the science and history of cheesemaking (caseology), the study of the planet Earth (geology), and the study and biology of ocean creatures (marine biology). I also interviewed Shawn Bath, a cleanupologist; he'll teach us about respecting our world's oceans. We'll explore the science and study of bees (apiology) and talk to a beekeeper. Then we'll finish by diving into the study of ancient life (paleontology).

You'll find games, experiments, drawing prompts, and recipes, and there are no rules or particular ways to read this book. You can start at the beginning or the end, or skip around to the parts that interest you. At the back of the book, you'll find definitions and a list of books and movies you can read and watch if you're interested in learning about other ologies. In no time at all, you'll be wandering around, exploring, having fun, observing, and asking yourself, "IsThisAnOlogy?"

Are you ready to start learning?

Science is such an adventure!

ORNITHOLOGY

Hello everybody! Or should I say, "tweet, tweet!" or "whoo, whoo!"
I'm so excited to teach you about **ornithology**! Ornithology means the scientific study of birds!

An ornithologist is a person who studies birds. That might mean they look at the behaviour of birds, but it could also mean that they study the bodies of birds or their homes. They might do research, lead tours, or spend time watching the ways birds live together. An ornithologist is always on an adventure!

Q & A WITH AN ORNITHOLOGIST

Laura King is an ornithologist working and living in St. John's, Newfoundland and Labrador, Canada. Her job is fascinating; she gets to spend time in nature, observing birds, and educating people on how they can help their feathered friends.

LET'S CHAT WITH LAURA AND FIND OUT MORE!

? Laura, how did you become an ornithologist?

" When I was younger, I was interested in all living things. I started to read articles about wildlife and conservation and realized that even though I didn't know any biologists, people seemed to be working with birds as their job, so maybe I could do that too when I grew up. After many years of university, I eventually ended up specializing in understanding how humans affect the health and conservation of birds.

? How can a person study birds?

" Anyone can study birds! Your most important tools are your senses—your eyes and your ears. With those, you can learn how birds find their homes, communicate with each other, find food, and care for their babies. Just like humans, birds have languages. To study bird behaviour, we can learn some of their languages too, and then we can hear the differences between a romantic song, a call to warn other birds, and even a bird fight.

Not all ornithologists work outside. Museums and laboratories are great places to conduct research! A museum's collection can help us understand how birds have changed over time and even let us study extinct birds. When we need to study samples we have taken from birds or their habitats, we use laboratories that can analyze DNA and pollution or other things we might want to measure that affect birds. We are still learning new ways to study birds, and new technologies that we can use are continuously developed.

? What kind of tools do you use?

" Binoculars are #1!

You can also add special bird telescopes, a bird blind (a structure that lets us study birds quite closely without being seen), audio and video recorders, and more. The most powerful tool of all? Using your own senses to observe birds!

Sometimes I've had to capture a bird to study it safely, so I've used traps, poles with loops, or special thin nets. We often want to know where birds go, so we use bird bands to find out. These are small metal rings that fit precisely to the bird's leg—sort of like a piece of jewellery for the bird. We have attached tiny transmitters on these bird bands to send the data back to our laptops, showing us where they are worldwide. We can use boats, helicopters, and climbing equipment to get to where the birds live. I even study birds by kayak and canoe sometimes!

❓ What's your favourite thing about ornithology?

❝ My favourite part of ornithology involves noticing new things. I've watched a baby seabird use its beak to break out of its egg, and I've seen a kingfisher dip down to fish in an urban river near my house. Learning to see and hear all the birds—hundreds of different kinds, wherever you live—is a memorable experience and something anyone can do.

❓ What's your favourite piece of trivia about birds?

❝ Well, I love dinosaurs, so one of my favourite pieces of trivia is something you might have heard before—birds are dinosaurs!

But wait, didn't the dinosaurs disappear? Yes! Most of the dinosaurs did go extinct, but at that time, more than a hundred million years ago, some birds made it through and eventually evolved into the thousands of modern bird species we see today. So, watching a bird in your backyard, you're looking at a dino. If you see their scaly feet up close someday, you'll think you're looking at a reptile—and you will be!

One of the neatest things about birds is that each species looks unique!

Plumage is a layer of feathers that covers a bird. Ornithologists study the pattern, arrangement, and colour of these feathers, because plumage can give clues about how birds protect themselves, attract a mate, and reduce friction when they fly through the air or float on the water.

BIRD OF PARADISE

Some birds have bright, vivid plumage—like the show-stopping bird of paradise. It's stunning: green, red, and blue! Other birds, like the American duck, have evolved to hide and blend in with their habitat, so their feathers are grey and brown.

My favourite bird is the Atlantic puffin! It spends time on the rocky shores of Newfoundland each summer. To me, Atlantic puffins look like tiny clowns—their plumage is black and orange.

Did you know that a group of puffins is called a **circus**?

What's your favourite bird?

ATLANTIC PUFFIN

IF YOU WANT TO KNOW MORE ABOUT THE OCEAN HABITAT WHERE MANY BIRDS LIVE, SKIP AHEAD TO THE CHAPTER ON MARINE BIOLOGY ON PAGE 27!

AMERICAN DUCK

Some ornithologists study where birds live.
Birds are found on every continent in the world! Some of our feathered friends live in the driest, dustiest deserts, and others live in our frozen polar regions. Some build nests in tall treetops, and others hide their homes in deep, dark caves.

CHECK OUT THE MAP ON PAGE 9 AND SEE WHERE DIFFERENT BIRDS MAKE THEIR HOMES.

The Arctic tern is the only bird that visits all seven continents. It has a long **migration**!

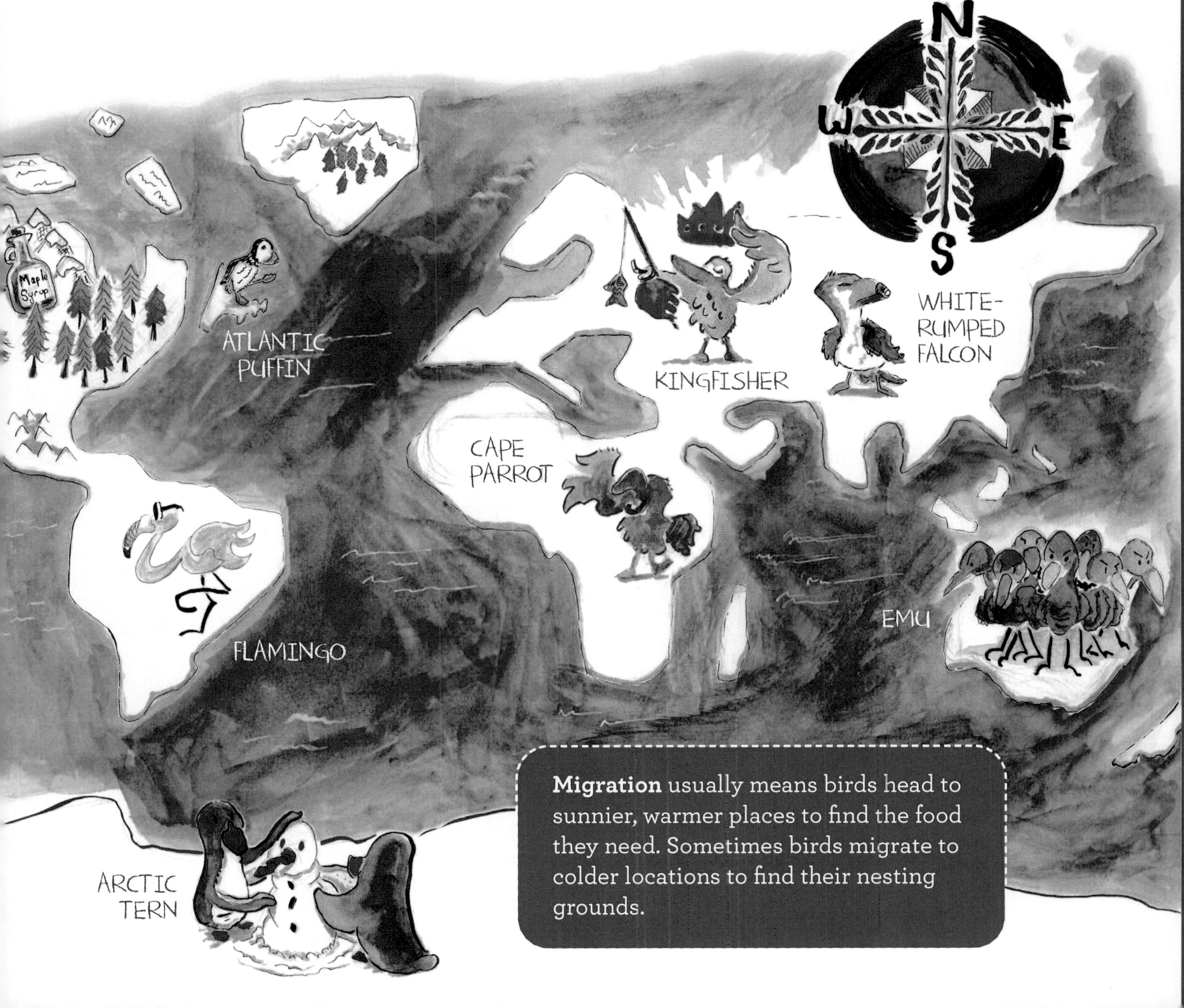
N
W
E
S
Maple Syrup
ATLANTIC PUFFIN
KINGFISHER
WHITE-RUMPED FALCON
CAPE PARROT
FLAMINGO
EMU
ARCTIC TERN

Migration usually means birds head to sunnier, warmer places to find the food they need. Sometimes birds migrate to colder locations to find their nesting grounds.

Birds are the best, huh? It's fun to appreciate birds, but we shouldn't touch them, disturb them, or even get too close. There's a common myth that bird parents will abandon their young if we get near. The real danger is that human activity around a nest can attract predators and draw attention to the baby birds!

Instead, you can observe them from a distance with a pair of binoculars or listen to their different songs. This is a hobby called *birding*; scientists also observe birds when conducting research, so birding is a great way to practise your science skills.

Bird watch trip
Great plumage,
Beautiful voice.
10/10

Have you ever heard of the Christmas Bird Count? Taking place in December each year, the Christmas Bird Count is North America's longest-running citizen science project. A citizen science project is one where non-scientists (like you!) can help gather information, and later scientists analyze the data.

The data collected is shared by researchers, conservationists, universities, and wildlife agencies, giving them a picture of the long-term health of different bird populations across North America. The Christmas Bird Count is a really important tool!

You can sign up for the Christmas Bird Count online by reaching out to the Audubon Society. In the meantime, you can practise birding by keeping these tips in mind!

TIPS

→ Habitat is a very important part of identifying unknown birds. Where are you? Right now, I'm near the waterfront in a city, so I'm probably not going to see a great horned owl, but I could see pigeons, gulls, and terns.

→ Listening is as important as looking! Remember that small birds tend to have high- pitched songs, while a larger bird like a raven might sound low and croaky. A great way to practise identifying birds through song is to listen to recordings online.

→ If you're using your eyes, remember to look at the plumage; this will give you clues as to what bird you're watching. Are there markings on the wings? What colour is the bird's chest? These details will help you identify the bird species.

→ Go slow! You can't learn to identify birds quickly— you have to have patience and you have to learn slow, but I promise it'll be worth it! Birding is like being on a never-ending scavenger hunt!

CHECK OUT THE GLOSSARY AT THE BACK OF THE BOOK IF YOU WANT TO LEARN MORE ABOUT THE ORIGINS OR MEANINGS OF THE WORDS.

CASEOLOGY

Caseology is the study of cheese and cheesemaking! It's arguably the most delicious of the *ologies*. While most of our *ologies* can be found in the dictionary, the word caseology is new and it's made up of the Latin word for cheese (*caseus*) and the Greek suffix for a branch of study (*logia*)! It's a word used by some people in the food industry.

Cheese is food made from milk. You might have tasted some of the most common types, like mozzarella, cheddar, Swiss, and American cheese. Did you know that cheesemakers have developed over 1800 types of cheese? Sometimes cheese is named for the country or town where it was first created.

Cheese is often put into categories by caseologists and cheesemakers; the category depends on the following factors:

DAIRY ANIMALS Cheese is often made from the milk of cows, sheep, or goats, but some cheese comes from other animals, like buffalo, water buffalo, yaks, and camels.

AGE Some cheese is made to be eaten fresh and can be enjoyed immediately. Aging gives cheese many fascinating tastes and textures. Aged cheese is usually harder than fresh, softer cheese. Sometimes aged cheese develops mould—a kind that is safe to eat.

FLAVOUR The way that cheese tastes is described from mild to sharp. The next time you try cheese, really think about it, and try your best to explain it. Observing is part of being an *ologist*.

TEXTURE The feel of a cheese ranges from soft to hard. Soft cheeses are creamy and easily spread on other food. Hard cheeses have less water, so they must be sliced or grated to be eaten or added to recipes.

One family of cheesemakers (the Johanssons of Sweden) make the most expensive cheese in the world—from moose milk! Moose are large animals that live in the wild, so milking a moose takes a calm and gentle hand. The three moose sisters—Gullan, Haelga and Juno—only lactate from May to September. The family makes four types of moose cheese from their limited milk supply. If you crave a taste of this rare treat, the price can be up to $1,000 for a kilo of moose cheese. Wow!

CAN YOU MAKE A LIST OF ALL THE TYPES OF CHEESE THAT YOU'VE HEARD OF? THEN ASK YOUR FRIENDS AND FAMILY TO SEE IF THEY CAN ADD TO YOUR LIST.

Archaeology is another *ology*; it's the study of human history. Archaeologists are scientists who look for proof of how people lived by digging for things that were left behind and finding items that were lost and buried. Scientists use what they learn to propose theories or explanations about life in the past. They discovered prehistoric pottery shards in Libya that held traces of milk. Based on their discoveries, they estimate that people started making cheese at least 8000 years ago.

No one knows exactly how cheese was invented, but it was probably an accidental discovery. Archaeologists think that certain cultures kept dairy animals and would get more milk from their animals than they could drink. After the invention of pottery, they stored milk in clay containers. When left for a long time in a warm place, the milk started to break down. Imagine their surprise when the milk had changed into delicious cheese!

Another theory is that people from ancient cultures salted their milk to help it keep longer. That salt would eventually lead the milk to become cheese. Or they may have accidentally combined milk and fruit juice. The acid in the fruit would curdle the milk.

There's evidence that cheese was enjoyed in Europe, Central Asia, the Middle East, and even the dry, dusty Sahara Desert!

In cooler climates—for example, in northern Europe—you don't need to use as much salt to make cheese! The colder temperatures mean that microbes can live in milk for months and even years. Microbes are teeny living things, too small to see without a microscope, that do all kinds of jobs. One is to help turn milk into cheese. Caves were often used to store cheese because their cool temperatures kept the good microbes growing steadily!

Curdling is when milk separates into two parts—curds (solids) and whey (liquid). This can happen slowly and naturally as the milk warms and starts to spoil. We can make it happen faster by adding an acid, like vinegar or lemon juice, to the milk. When the milk curdles, you can press out the liquid and add salt to make it last longer and taste good.

"You Banbury cheese!" — William Shakespeare used this insult in his comedy *The Merry Wives of Windsor* (1597).

William Shakespeare was a famous playwright in England in the late 1500s and early 1600s. He wrote over 39 plays and 150 poems and mentioned cheese in many of his productions! Before Shakespeare, cheese was associated with life on the road, and with people who would travel the countryside looking for work. Shakespeare's plays helped make cheese more popular. He was like a modern-day social media influencer. Shakespeare was very well-loved, so his large audiences would learn about new things from him and want to experience them too. He started a trend by mentioning cheese in his writings.

Banbury cheese is named for the town in England where the cheese was made. Aged cheese usually develops a hard exterior, or rind, and when the rind was peeled off, there was just a thin strip of cheese left behind. Banbury cheese was well known as a thin cheese. Shakespeare used this phrase to describe a character who was either very slim or they were shallow on the inside.

Understanding the history of cheese is an important part of being a caseologist or cheesemaker! Cheese shows up A LOT in popular culture, books, history, and stories. Do you know this nursery rhyme?

Little Miss Muffet
Sat on a tuffet,
Eating her curds and whey;
Along came a spider,
Who sat down beside her
And frightened Miss Muffet away.

This nursery rhyme first appeared in a book in 1805! We don't know who wrote it, but most of us still learn this rhyme today. Curds and whey were a popular cheese snack that people ate, in the same way that people eat cottage cheese or yogurt today.

15

YOU CAN BE A CHEESEMAKER!

Making simple cheeses is easy and fun! For today's recipe, we're going to be using the stove, so you'll need to get help from an adult. It will take about 30 minutes to make the cheese and an hour to let it firm up.

You'll need the following:

4 cups whole milk

3 tablespoons white vinegar (or lemon or lime juice)

A mesh strainer

A pot

Cheesecloth

CHEESE CAN BE YUMMY AND HEALTHY! IT'S TIME WE MADE SOME HOMEMADE CHEESE!

1. With an adult, heat 4 cups of whole milk on medium heat on the stovetop; do not boil. Slowly add the white vinegar, 1 tablespoon at a time; then stir, add the next tablespoon, and stir again. Once all the vinegar has been added, the curds will start to separate quickly! Remove from heat, cover the pot, and let sit for 15 minutes to complete the separation process.

2. While your cheese cools, line a mesh strainer with 2 layers of cheesecloth and place it over another bowl or large measuring cup to catch the liquid.

3. After 15 minutes, use a skimmer to ladle the curds out of the pot and into the cheesecloth. Twist the fabric together at the top, squeezing all the liquid from this cheese ball.

At this point, you may want to open it, add some salt, and squeeze again. When no more liquid comes out, tie a quick knot in the cheesecloth and leave for 1 hour in the strainer to allow the cheese to form a ball. Yum!

4 Open it up and remove the cheese. It's ready to serve.

This cheese is even more delicious if you add salt and any kind of herbs that you like! I love chopped dill, but caraway seeds, basil, and oregano also taste great! Sprinkle it into the cheese and stir with a spoon to mix.

There are many ways to use the leftover whey from making cheese, so don't toss it out!

Here are some ideas:

- Feed it to your dogs or any farm animals.

- Add it to baked goods that you make with your family.

- Make smoothies by adding ingredients you love.

- Water your acid-loving plants, like tomatoes or blueberries, with it.

- Pour it into your compost.

IF YOU ENJOY MAKING TASTY TREATS, SKIP TO THE CHAPTER ON APIOLOGY ON PAGE 35!

Did you know that five categories describe the flavours we taste? Sweet, sour, salty, bitter, and *umami*. Scientists named the flavour umami in 2002, but it was first used in Japan in 1908 to describe foods with a meaty, earthy, or savoury taste. Can you think of foods that fit into those five categories? Cakes are sweet, lemons are sour, French fries are salty, onions are bitter, and mushrooms and cheese are umami.

We don't just taste food with our mouths. We enjoy food most when several senses are engaged. Try this quick experiment to see how food tastes better when we see it, smell it, and taste it! First, pop a piece of cheese into your mouth with your eyes closed! Pretty tasty, huh? Now, with the second piece of cheese, use your sense of sight to look at the colour and shape of the cheese! How would you describe it? Now smell it! Sniff! What does it remind you of? Finally, eat it slowly. Close your lips and let it melt on your tongue! I bet that second piece was tastier! Understanding flavour is a big part of caseology!

GEOLOGY

Geology is the study of the Earth and how it changes. Geologists are scientists who study how the Earth began, what it is made of, and how it evolves over time. Some geologists are curious about the changes that cause disruptions like earthquakes, floods, or volcanoes. The earth is constantly changing, so there is a lot to learn about the history, the present, and what is yet to come for our planet!

Some geologists study the minerals we take from the earth to make things and some study how different types of rocks are formed.

A **mineral** is a solid substance created naturally with no outside help. Gold, iron, and copper are minerals. Gems are pieces of mineral cut into shapes and then polished and shined to show off their beauty. The diamonds and rubies in a ring or a necklace are the hardest minerals on earth.

A **rock** is usually made up of two or more minerals combined during a geological process like the ones described on the following pages. Granite is a hard rock and talc is a soft rock.

Did you know that glacier ice is also a rock? It's made entirely of snowflakes, which are six-sided crystals.

Geologists who study the rocks, minerals, and formations on top of and below the earth's surface can find clues about the Earth's history. There are three main types of rocks, and their names are based on how they were formed. Ready for some super-quick experiments?

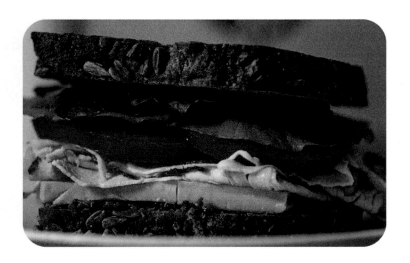

Sedimentary rocks are formed when **sediments**—sands, small rocks, and plants—settle in layers in the water and on land, like the way the dust settles on a table. Many different layers settle and build up over time. These kinds of rocks almost look like a sandwich. Make a sandwich with cheese, lettuce, tomato, and turkey inside! That's what sedimentary rock looks like. Don't eat it yet; keep reading.

Metamorphic rocks are made when an existing rock is changed by heat or pressure. These rocks have the same material as before, but they take up less or different space in their new form. A good way to picture this is to take your sedimentary sandwich and grill it with an adult. After it's heated, get an adult to cut it in half. Add pressure by pushing it down with a spatula and see how it changes shape. Once it cools, it can't return to the way it was before. All the same stuff is in there, but it's changed now. That's how these rocks are formed.

Igneous rocks form when lava, or hot, liquid rock, cools and becomes solid. With an adult, put some chocolate chips or a piece of chocolate in a microwave, heat it for about two minutes, then pour it out on a cookie sheet. When it cools, the chocolate is in a completely different shape than before. Now you can eat your sandwich and have some chocolate for dessert. You'll need that fuel to keep going through this book!

When scientists talk about the beginnings of planet Earth, the numbers seem so big. The Earth started forming over 4 billion years ago. It took about 700 million years to develop the solid crust we know as the land.

Here's a great way to visualize a long timeline. Try it out.

Stretch your arms out from your sides and look in a mirror. If your arm span is the timeline of the earth's formation, your right fingertips are the earth's formation. Then look all the way over to your left wrist; this was when prehistoric life began, and lots of changes happened. The age of dinosaurs happened across the first two knuckles of your left hand. Today is the age of mammals, which would be your left hand's fingertips. Human beings are at the very tip of your left fingernails. Isn't it wild that people have only existed for a short time?

IF YOU WANT TO SEE A DETAILED DESCRIPTION OF THE AGES OF THE EARTH, SKIP TO THE CHAPTER ON PALEONTOLOGY ON PAGE 46!

Q & A WITH A GEOLOGIST

Opeyemi Jaunty-Aidamenbor studied geology and mineral science in Nigeria and is now doing interdisciplinary post-graduate studies in St. John's, Newfoundland, Canada. She knows so much about the Earth and how it was formed!

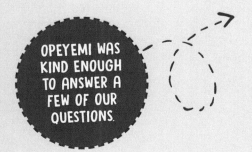

OPEYEMI WAS KIND ENOUGH TO ANSWER A FEW OF OUR QUESTIONS.

? **Opeyemi, when and why did you first become interested in geology?**

" I became interested in geology when I was in high school. I enjoyed reading about hot springs, geysers, and canyons in my geography textbook and developed a curiosity to know more about the earth. Also, a geologist, one of my uncles, once took me to Olode village, Ibadan, south-western Nigeria, where valuable solid minerals were dug from the earth. I was intrigued! Some of the minerals mined from there include beryl, columbite, feldspar, mica, tantalite, and tourmaline.

? **What is an interesting geological experience that you have had?**

" I travelled to Erin Ijesa in Nigeria to view a majestic seven-step waterfall called the Olumirin waterfalls.

❓ Can you tell us about the minerals found in Newfoundland and Labrador?

❝ This place has many minerals, including quartz, feldspar, iron ore, tungsten, and uranium, among other rare earth and industrial minerals.

❓ What's your favourite thing you learned about the Earth?

❝ While studying geology at the university, I learned that, about 525 million years ago, the continents were all one piece and, according to a theory called plate tectonics, they split into the different parts that exist today—the continents can fit reasonably well together, like pieces of a puzzle. Then, in a process named continental drift, they slowly moved to where they are now.

❓ What's an interesting fact about the geology of Newfoundland and Labrador?

❝ Newfoundland and Labrador have a world-class geologically diverse landscape that attracts scientists from all over the world. For example, Gros Morne National Park in western Newfoundland has been described as the eighth wonder of the world because it proved that the continents drifted apart. At Gros Morne, you can walk over the ancient sea floor.

Most geologists agree that a mountain is a landform that rises at least 300 metres above its surrounding area. Mountains are mostly underground. Just like we only see the tip of an iceberg because most of it is underwater, the roots of a mountain go deep down into the earth. Neat, huh?

These five mountains are famous for their one-of-a-kind features and are celebrated places where geologists study.

MOUNT EVEREST lies on the border of the countries of Nepal and China in the Himalayan mountain range. Over the years, this mountain has become well-known because so many people try to climb to the top. When you look at it, it's easy to see that the mountain is triangular on all three sides.

Geologists think that Everest started to form over 40 million years ago. It is the highest mountain in the world at 8,849 metres (29,032 feet), according to the most recent measurements in 2020. The movement of the Earth is still pushing the mountain towards the sky. Using measuring devices, scientists now know that it rises about half a centimetre each year. So even at that age, Mount Everest is still growing!

The **GRAND CANYON** in Colorado was carved by erosion from the Colorado River about 6 million years ago.

It's easy to forget that the Grand Canyon is part of a mountain, but its peaks and plateaus, or high flat tops, are visible from above. The sedimentary rock formations are easily visible, but the oldest rocks at the base are metamorphic rocks with igneous rocks mixed in. Those rocks at the bottom of the canyon are named the Vishnu Basement Rocks.

Did you know that as long as water flows, the Grand Canyon's shape will keep changing?

The **ZHANGJIAJIE MOUNTAINS** are in Hunan province, central China. About 1.5 billion years ago, a volcano in the seabed erupted and became the base of a sandstone forest made from pillars. Sea erosion started over 380 million years ago and helped shape these unique towers that climb up high into a foggy sky. This is a fascinating site for everyone, especially geologists!

MOUNT RORAIMA is the highest tabletop mountain in South America, and it borders three countries—Venezuela, Guyana, and Brazil. It was formed when a large piece of flat land was forced upwards as the South American and African continents separated in a big geological shift over 180 million years ago. The mountain is 14 km long and 2810 metres high. The heavy rain on the plateau causes high waterfalls to drop over the edge.

MOUNT FUJI is the highest mountain in Japan at 3776 metres. It is known for its cone shape and snow-capped peak. It is an active volcano, but it has not erupted since the year 1707. Its picture-perfect look has made it one of the most recognizable places in the world.

MARINE BIOLOGY

Our next *ology* is **marine biology**. The word **marine** means of or about the ocean. **Biology** means the science of life and living things. So marine biology means the study of life in the oceans.

A marine biologist might work in a laboratory, but they could work on the water too. They research and study how the fishing industry, plastics, and climate change affect Earth's oceans. A marine biologist could study tiny, invisible plants or giant, awe-inspiring blue whales. Marine biology is so exciting!

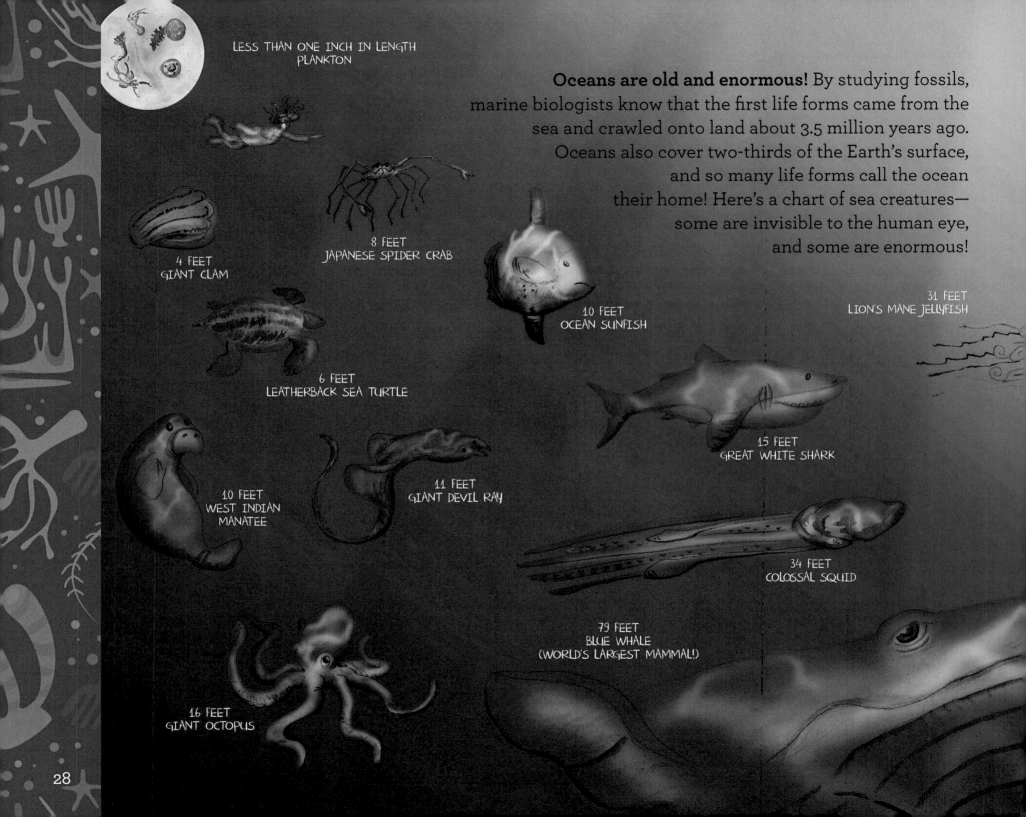

LESS THAN ONE INCH IN LENGTH
PLANKTON

Oceans are old and enormous! By studying fossils, marine biologists know that the first life forms came from the sea and crawled onto land about 3.5 million years ago. Oceans also cover two-thirds of the Earth's surface, and so many life forms call the ocean their home! Here's a chart of sea creatures— some are invisible to the human eye, and some are enormous!

4 FEET
GIANT CLAM

8 FEET
JAPANESE SPIDER CRAB

10 FEET
OCEAN SUNFISH

31 FEET
LION'S MANE JELLYFISH

6 FEET
LEATHERBACK SEA TURTLE

15 FEET
GREAT WHITE SHARK

10 FEET
WEST INDIAN
MANATEE

11 FEET
GIANT DEVIL RAY

34 FEET
COLOSSAL SQUID

79 FEET
BLUE WHALE
(WORLD'S LARGEST MAMMAL!)

16 FEET
GIANT OCTOPUS

Whoa. Did you know that humans have only explored about 5 per cent of the ocean? Just imagine the funny creatures we still haven't even met yet!

GRAB SOME PAPER AND DRAW YOUR OWN! A BIG PART OF SCIENCE IS USING YOUR IMAGINATION AND BEING CURIOUS ABOUT POSSIBILITIES!

Maybe they have twelve eyes and glowing bellies. Or possibly there's a small, sleek deep-sea whale that's managed to escape being seen by scientists. There's so much left to discover! I've drawn some made-up sea animals.

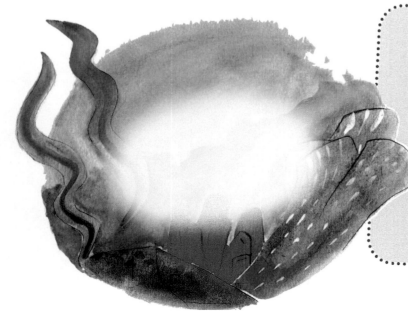

Did you know that all of our oceans are connected? It's true! They make up one giant body of salt water. Scientists organize them into five different sections, which we call the Pacific Ocean, the Atlantic Ocean, the Indian Ocean, the Southern Ocean, and the Arctic Ocean. They do this because the oceans are quite different, with unique weather patterns, tides, plants, and animals.

The giant squid is a **cephalopod**! Cephalopods are a type of mollusc. They have a large brain and no backbone, and they're considered intelligent. One thing most cephalopods have in common is an ink sac. If they are scared or attacked, the giant squid will squirt dark ink into the water. This confuses creatures that might want to snack on the squid, and it can make a quick getaway! Marine biologists are fascinated by squid ink, and some studies show that this ink might have valuable applications for humans.

The giant squid is my favourite ocean creature. They live in the darkest crevices of the deep ocean. Scientists have trouble observing them in their natural habitat. Still, a few specimens have washed up on the beaches of Newfoundland and Labrador, which is exciting because almost everything we know about the giant squid comes from studying the bodies that have washed ashore.

Giant squids can grow to be 1000 pounds! They have eight arms and two long tentacles. Their eyes are enormous—bigger than any other animal's—and their tentacles are covered in suckers, which they use to catch jellyfish! Scientists measure the squid's mantle and beak and examine all parts to understand how they move and survive in the depths.

NL TIMES

Giant Squid visits topsail beach—

Interview with sea captain says the squid was sun bathing when he asked the cephalopod for an autograph. —more on page 8

You've probably heard that our oceans are in trouble. That's true. There are many threats to our world's oceans. Climate change means water temperatures are rising, and the sea is becoming more acidic. Acids or acidic water is hard on the shells of animals, clams, oysters, and mussels, which are already having a harder time keeping their shells intact. It doesn't look good for coral reefs either; marine biologists are discovering that many reef systems are collapsing. Humans have overfished some species, which can be a big problem for the food chain; suddenly, some fish find themselves having to swim farther and expend more energy in the hunt for food. We're also leaving fishing nets in the water too long, and those catch young fish before they've had a chance to reproduce. Ocean pollution, fishing nets left in the oceans, and plastics are enormous problems, but luckily, we can do something to help!

Q & A WITH AN CLEANUPOLOGIST

You've probably heard of someone being a marine biologist, but have you heard of a cleanupologist? *Cleanupologist* is a word I just made up! It means someone committed to studying the mess in our oceans and to cleaning it up. It's a little different from a marine biologist!

Meet Shawn Bath. Shawn is a deep-sea diver and famous cleanupologist from Newfoundland and Labrador. He and his crew spend time leading clean-ups, diving for garbage, and teaching people about the importance of protecting our oceans.

? **How did you become passionate about saving the oceans?**

" I spent 21 years diving for sea urchins, and I swam over the trash every day and didn't have time to do anything about it when I was working, but one day I decided I had to do something.

? **What's at the bottom of the bays and harbours in Newfoundland?**

" The bottoms of harbours are littered with thousands of bottles, cans, chip bags, tires, numerous batteries, and abandoned fishing gear. Our harbours are much like the internet; anything you can imagine, it's there.

? **What can kids do to help protect and clean up our oceans?**

" I tell people to stop buying single-use plastics. Try to buy things that last. I also want to encourage kids not to litter. Most importantly, kids can organize beach clean-ups too!

? **What's next for you and your team of cleanupologists?**

" We're hoping to increase the number of our crews. We want to have more folks removing trash so we lessen our impact on the ocean. It's time to heal it. We try to understand why people pollute and convince people to join in our efforts.

I'VE SHARED SOME TIPS BELOW. BEACH CLEAN-UPS ARE ESSENTIAL.

BEACH CLEAN-UP FOR KIDS

PICK A BEACH! Shawn Bath says that some beaches are called "collector beaches," meaning that tides push plastic and ocean garbage onto the shore. A cleanupologist like Shawn can walk along a beach and quickly discover if it needs a clean-up. He observes and looks for garbage. You can do the same! A collector beach is a great one to choose! But you can pick any beach you love and want to clean up.

PICK A DATE! The start of the summer is an excellent time of year to organize a beach clean-up.

You'll need the following:
A first-aid kit
Reusable gloves
Reusable water bottles
Hand sanitizer
Sunscreen
Bug spray
Volunteers to help you

GET PERMISSION! Cleaning the beach is kind, but you should still ask permission from the people in charge. The grown-ups in your life can email the city or town where it's located or check in with the local police.

GET VOLUNTEERS! Many people want to help but don't always know where to start. Call around, ask your friends, and spread the word. Social media is a great way to organize a beach clean-up!

GATHER YOUR SUPPLIES! Make sure to bring everything on the list on page 33! You want people to wear gloves when handling garbage. Since people volunteer their time, offering them sunscreen, bug spray, and water is kind. A local business may donate these things to your group if you ask them to help.

HAVE FUN! Play music, have conversations, and turn the clean-up into a fun get-together. If people have fond memories of your beach clean-up, they'll be more likely to organize one of their own or come back next year!

SHARE YOUR STORY! Take pictures of your clean-up and share them! Tell people about your clean-up afterward! The more people cleaning up our beaches and removing plastic from the ocean, the better!

IF YOU WANT TO KNOW MORE ABOUT OCEANS AND THE EARTH WE CALL HOME, CHECK OUT THE CHAPTER ON GEOLOGY ON PAGE 19!

APIOLOGY

Buzz, buzz! It's time to talk about bees! The scientific study of bees, especially honeybees, is called **apiology**.

Bees belong to a large group of creatures called insects. Since there are so many kinds of insects, scientists have broken the groups into families and given them names, just like you have a family name. Bees are part of the **Apoidea** family, which includes honeybees and bumblebees. You can usually tell them apart by looking closely at them.

Bumblebees have thick bodies, dark wings, and a lot of hair. Honeybees are thinner, less hairy, and have four wings. Bumblebees live in burrows or tunnels in the ground, while honeybees live in hives and trees.

BUMBLEBEE

HONEYBEE

An **apiologist** is a scientist who studies bees. Did you know that an apiarist is a person who keeps honeybees? We usually call them beekeepers. We're going to focus mostly on honeybees in this chapter because they are so crucial to our food cycle.

From studying bees, apiologists have learned that bees fly from flower to flower, collecting nectar to feed themselves and their colonies. At the same time, the bees do a second job, called pollination, that helps provide food for humans and other creatures.

You see, male flowers produce pollen, a fine, dusty powder that contains ingredients to make new flowers. Bees love all kinds of flowers, from roses to dandelions. Some flowers are male, some are female, and each contains different ingredients. Bees are sort of like a baker: they pick up ingredients and mix them, just like in a recipe, to make new flowers.

When a bee lands on a male flower, pollen sticks to the bee's fuzzy feet. Once the bee has sipped up the nectar, it zips over to a nearby flower. When the bee lands on a female flower close by, the male pollen gets mixed in with the female ingredients, and that's when new life begins. This process is called **pollination**. Once a flower is pollinated, it has everything it needs to create new fruit or vegetables, and that fruit carries new seeds!

When those fruits get eaten by other creatures, they leave behind some or all of the seeds. In time, many of those seeds will reach the soil. New plants will grow, and the food cycle will start again.

IT'S TIME TO EXPERIMENT! LET'S LEARN MORE ABOUT POLLINATION ON PAGE 38!

LET'S LEARN ABOUT POLLINATION!

You'll need the following:

1 cotton ball or colourful pom

Glue

Icing sugar

4 pieces of construction paper

Pencil and scissors

1. Draw a large flower on each sheet of construction paper. Be sure the flowers have a circle in the middle of the petals. Cut out your hand-drawn flowers and line the flowers up in a row. Dab the centres with glue.

2. Carefully sprinkle some icing sugar into the middle of the first flower. This represents the flower's pollen. Using your cotton ball or pom, pretend it is a bee and "land" in the

middle of the first flower filled with icing sugar (pollen). See how some sugar sticks to it? Don't dust it off.

3 Now, "fly" your cotton ball or pom to the middle of the second, the third, and the fourth flower. See how a pollinator leaves bits of sugar (pollen) in each flower and picks up new pollen? In nature, every flower has some pollen. While the bees leave pollen behind, they pick up more pollen from the new flower and take it to the next one. Pollination is how flowers, fruits, plants, and trees grow and spread!

4 When you're all done, be sure to clean up. Don't keep this sugar around because it'll attract bugs and small rodents that you won't want in your home.

Honey is such a superfood! It has antibacterial and antiviral properties to help you fight off sickness. You can drink a spoonful of honey to relieve a cough, or you can put honey on a cut or sore to help it heal faster. Honey can last hundreds of years without spoiling, but only if it's kept sealed and nothing is added to it.

Did you know that humans have been eating honey for thousands of years? Ancient art found in Africa, Europe, Asia, and Australia shows humans collecting honey. Some of this art dates back 40,000 years. Archaeologists have found honey in an ancient Egyptian tomb, and it was still perfectly good to eat!

Honeybees only live for about 6 weeks, but they get a lot done in that short time! A bee will visit 50 to 100 flowers on a single trip out of the hive. Each trip takes about 30 to 60 minutes, and each honeybee makes about 10 trips per day. One bee could visit up to 1000 flowers per day. They are, quite literally, busy bees!

Apiologists have learned that bees need both nectar and pollen to make honey. Bees suck up the nectar into a bag on their bellies and bring it home. Then, the worker bees at the hive collect the nectar through their mouths. The nectar is passed this way, from bee to bee, until it gets to the honeycomb to be stored. As the nectar is passed along, the bee's wings flap to dry it out, so most of the water disappears. This leaves only the sticky, sweet liquid that we know as honey. Each honeybee makes about 1 tablespoon of honey in its lifetime.

Bees survive the winter by eating their honey, but they don't need much of it! Beekeepers only take the honey that the bees do not need!

Some people are scared of bees, mainly because they have a unique way of protecting themselves. If you get too close to a beehive or step on a bee, its instinct is to defend itself. When bees feel threatened, one of the ways they protect themselves is by stinging.

Honey has a long history! Archaeologists have learned that in Egypt, 5000 years ago, honey was the primary sweetener used in cooking and baking. And 2000 years ago, people offered honey to the gods and the spirits of their dead loved ones. In Germany, in the eleventh century, it was so prized that peasants paid part of their rent to their landlords in honey and beeswax.

Apiologists often examine hives to determine the social structure of bees. **Apiarists** (bee-keepers) also spend a lot of time around hives, but they are more concerned with gathering honey, so they wear special clothes to protect themselves from stings.

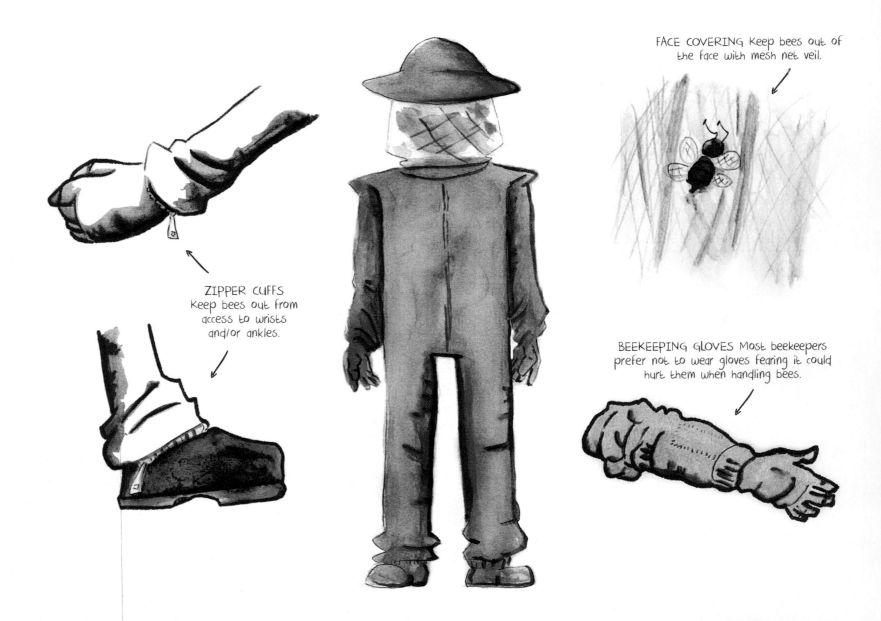

FACE COVERING Keep bees out of the face with mesh net veil.

ZIPPER CUFFS Keep bees out from access to wrists and/or ankles.

BEEKEEPING GLOVES Most beekeepers prefer not to wear gloves fearing it could hurt them when handling bees.

Q&A WITH AN APIARIST

LET'S CHAT ABOUT APIOLOGY WITH MEGAN SAMMS!

? How did you first get interested in beekeeping?

" I got interested in keeping and tending to bees when I worked at a small farmers' market in New Brunswick. I was spending time on different organic farms. I learned that if it weren't for pollinators, like bees, we would have less than one third of the food crops (grown in gardens and growing in the wild) that we're used to eating. So my love for bees exploded!

I wanted to study with someone before I took on the responsibility of caring for 80,000 bee lives. I found a mentor, someone who would give me hands-on experience, a short time later in Treaty 8 territory, near Lesser Slave Lake. I learned from and worked with Gereon Hoentgesberg for several years. He taught me how to breed bees, care for them, and harvest honey, pollen, and wax. Bees are fascinating!! There is always more to learn about them, their role and impact, and their importance to all life. I will never know enough about them, and I'll certainly never know it all!

? What did you learn when you first started?

" It's helpful to work with a mentor when learning about bees. When I started beekeeping, I had Gereon by my side, and he caught my mistakes before I did. At first, I didn't know when to give bees more space, and they got a little cramped and produced less honey. But those things came with time, patience, and practice!

? What is your favourite part of the beekeeping process?

" The bees play a very active role at our farm. They pollinate our food crops; we plant nectar flowers specifically for them. I love how they help me think about the world as a well-connected living place. I love how they help me think about caretaking and how to do it well. Of course, we all love honey harvest time here—we taste-test a lot and keep samples from every year.

? How can kids help the bees?

" There are many things that a person of any age can do to help bees! Here are a few:

Learn about honeybee culture and how to identify them.

Don't squish them.

Plant nectar plants around your land base for bees. These could be sunflowers, sweet clover, red clover, or buckwheat.

Encourage wild and native plant species like fireweed, goldenrod, and aster to grow where you live. Dandelions are an essential early-season crop for honeybees and all pollinators!

Ask your guardians or parents not to cut their lawn! Many pollinators live on the same land as people. Maintaining their habitat is essential for the whole world.

> Honey is sweet, and lemons are sour. When we blend these flavours, we get a refreshing drink! Try this tasty recipe; it's so lovely on a summer day!

You'll need the following:

4 lemons

1/2 cup honey

1 quart boiling water

1/2 cup fresh mint

Optional:

3 tablespoons of dried lavender

HONEY LEMONADE

MAKES 4 1/2 CUPS OF LEMONADE

It might be a good idea to ask a grown-up to help you.

1. Wash your lemons and roll them between your hands: this is an excellent way to get more juice out of your citrus fruits.

2. Peel your lemons, and put the peels in a large bowl. Now cut the lemons in half and juice them. Make sure your lemon juice is in a separate bowl.

3. Add honey and the quart of boiling water to the bowl with the lemon peels. The hot water will make the lemon oil leave the peels.

4. Once this bowl of water is cool, take the peels out.

5. Now stir the lemon juice into the honey and water and garnish it with fresh mint or lavender. Put it in a jug in the fridge or add a few ice cubes to make it colder and more refreshing!

IF YOU WANT TO LEARN MORE ABOUT FLAVOUR, CHECK OUT THE CHAPTER ON CASEOLOGY ON PAGE 12!

PALEONTOLOGY

Many people think **paleontology** is the study of dinosaurs, but it *actually* means studying ancient life. That means that a paleontologist might be a person who studies the imprints of ancient germs, tiny fossils of fungi, the big bones of long-extinct mammals, or giant dinosaurs.

We only know a little about ancient life. We can imagine how the Earth looked billions of years ago, but mostly it's a mystery. Paleontologists act like detectives!

Fossils are the clues that paleontologists use to solve the mystery. And because of paleontologists, we're constantly learning more about ancient life.

Different *ologists* will often coordinate and conduct research together. Geologists and paleontologists are both interested in understanding how Earth, and the life on it, began so long ago.

These are the tools a paleontologist might use! Can you match the tool to its purpose?

Fossils are traces of ancient life that have been preserved in the earth for a long time. A brontosaurus leg bone is a fossil, but so is the tiniest imprint of a shell. Some paleontologists specialize in studying coprolites, which are fossilized poops!

LET'S CHAT ABOUT PALEONTOLOGY WITH ROD STEPHEN TAYLOR!

Q & A WITH A PALEONTOLOGIST

❓ How did you become a paleontologist? Was it a long journey?

❝ I studied—long and hard! I was inspired by paleontology as a child, as I grew up near Manuels River in Newfoundland, Canada, and collected trilobite fossils often throughout my youth. I always knew I wanted to be a biologist, and when I took a course in paleontology as an undergraduate student at university, I immediately knew I'd found my calling.

❓ Where do you usually work? Is it a lab? A site? What kind of tools do you use?

❝ Paleontology involves many kinds of research. Fieldwork is an essential component, while some research is done on collections in museums or universities. Sometimes we can collect fossils from the field, but not always. For these fossils, we do observational studies in the field (when the weather is good!) and we also work from photographs or make replicas using silicone and plaster. A lot of work is done on computers or in a library, as we must compare new fossils to living animals to understand them best—and this involves a lot of reading and writing.

What does a typical day on a site look like?

It depends on the site! For fossils like those at Mistaken Point in Newfoundland, fieldwork involves photography and using silicone resin to make replicas. Collecting fossils involves much different fieldwork: small fossils can be extracted using brushes, hammers, or rock saws and wrapped in paper or bubble wrap to protect them during transportation. Big fossils, like bones, may require being covered in plaster, moved by cranes, and transported on pallets to protect them while they are moved from the field to the lab.

What's your favourite thing about your job?

Discovery! When looking at fossils in the field or a lab, you never know when you will find something completely new to science—and there are no words to describe the thrill of finding something that no one has ever seen before. The opportunity to describe an organism for the first time is an incredible privilege.

What is the biggest misunderstanding about paleontology?

Probably that all paleontologists study dinosaurs. Life existed on the Earth for more than 300 million years before the first dinosaurs appeared. Most paleontologists have never worked on dinosaurs of any kind.

Dinosaur fossils have been found on every continent— even Antarctica! Canada, especially Newfoundland and Labrador, has some of the oldest fossils on the planet! This means that paleontologists from around the world come and study here!

? What's the best way for kids to learn about paleontology?

" There are so many ways! The internet is one precious resource: many websites are devoted to the history of life, animal and plant groups that have lived through the history of the Earth, the different geological periods in Earth's history, and how to recognize fossils. The list is endless! There are also many books devoted to paleontology, aimed at every level, from complete beginner to expert. On top of this, many wonderfully entertaining educational TV programs about paleontology consider every aspect of this field of science. There are also hundreds of educational centres worldwide that you can visit. You can talk to scientists and interpreters about the fascinating pieces of living history there. They are often easy to access, offering tours where visitors can look at fossils on display in exhibits and the field.

Long before people existed, the Earth was covered with other life forms! Most of these creatures are extinct now, but we can still learn about them through the study of paleontology and the works of paleontologists. The simplified chart on pages 52 and 53 explain the history of life on Earth—there are more categories than this, but it will help you get started.

ARCHEAN This is the first of the two formal divisions of Precambrian time. It's when the Earth was first formed! Can you imagine that far back? Was it all ocean? Was the air breathable? Some paleontologists try to answer these questions.

PRECAMBRIAN This period began about 4.6 billion years ago and ended about 542 million years ago! It includes the Archean (described above) and the Protozoic era. Some of the oldest plant fossils in the world are 1 billion years old. Interestingly, a team of international researchers concluded that fossils found at Mistaken Point, Newfoundland and Labrador, are the world's oldest evidence of animal life. They are about 574 million years old.

CAMBRIAN EXPLOSION The Cambrian period happened during the Paleozoic era and was a critical time in Earth's history. In the millennia before, organisms were simple bacteria. Bacteria are so small that we need a microscope to see them. During the Cambrian explosion, many new types of animals appeared in the fossil record. The fossil record means the history of life on the planet as documented by fossils! Paleontologists are still trying to figure out why so many forms of life appeared in a short time!

PALEOZOIC The first creatures to show up in the Paleozoic were arthropods! They would be distantly related to jellyfish and spiders. The Paleozoic period is also when the first fish showed up and when plants began to grow on land. Picture giant ferns waving in the wind and deep, boggy swamps! The Paleozoic era can be further divided into different time periods. The first of these was called the Cambrian period, and that's when those arthropods appeared.

MESOZOIC This was the time of the dinosaur. Dinosaurs roamed the Earth for a long time! This period began 251 million years ago and ended 65 million years ago. Some dinosaurs were plant-eaters, but others were predators and had fearsome teeth and sharp claws! Some dinosaurs lived on land, but others soared through the air on giant wings or swam in the ocean. Mammals evolved during the Mesozoic period, too. The first ones were tiny mouse-like creatures. Eventually, birds came onto the scene. But they didn't look like the birds we have now: they had massive teeth and claws. Paleontologists made these discoveries by comparing ancient fossils to today's mammals.

THE K–PG EXTINCTION EVENT About 66 million years ago, an asteroid hit the Earth and killed three-quarters of the plant and animal species. Some things did survive, like ancient sea turtles, crocodile relatives, and smallish mammals. Geologists and archaeologists worked together to develop the K-Pg theory. The impact site of the crater was discovered near Mexico, and the theory is credited to two scientists, Walter Alvarez and his father, Luis Alvarez.

THE CENOZOIC The Cenozoic is our current geological era! It started after the extinction event and continues today. This is when rhinos, hippos, horses, and all our favourite familiar animals first came onto the scene. Compared to dinosaurs, humans have only been around for a short period. Our ancestors, Hominins, first showed up about 4 million years ago. We're new here on Earth, but we're still responsible for taking care of it.

LET'S MAKE DINOSAUR BONES!

This craft will allow you to make *pretend* dinosaur bones. You can cover them with sand and use a tiny brush to clean the bones.

You'll need the following:

2 cups all-purpose flour
1 cup of salt
1 cup of water
Parchment paper
2 small paintbrushes
Dirt or sand

1. Mix the flour, salt, and water in a bowl. Stir with a spoon. Once the ingredients are mixed, remove them from the bowl and knead the dough. Kneading just means pushing the dough down onto a surface so the ingredients can come together. You push, press, and fold repeatedly—there's no right way to knead something. After a few minutes of kneading, you should be able to form shapes and use your dough like modelling clay.

Being a paleontologist must be cool, huh? We only know a little about what came before humans. Each day, for a paleontologist, must be filled with excitement and uncertainty. Imagine using a tiny brush to uncover a fossil! This is something a real-life paleontologist does. They use small chisels and brushes to carefully brush away other matter and reveal the rocks' fossils. They must move slowly and carefully, so take your time and pretend you're a paleontologist!

2 Now, make some bone shapes! Roll out your clay in a small, long cylinder for a leg bone. Have fun shaping it!

3 Once you are all done creating your bones, preheat your oven to 350°F. A grown-up should help with this part! Line a baking sheet with parchment. Set the bones you've made on the baking sheet, put them in the oven, and bake for 2 hours. They should be rock solid.

4 Once the bones are cool, it's time to play paleontologist! Place your bones in a big container. Cover them with sand or dirt. Now use your paintbrushes to gently brush away the dirt from your bones!

When paleontologists study fossils, they use two different techniques to determine the age of the fossil. These methods are called *relative dating* and *absolute dating*. Relative dating involves comparing the fossil to similar fossils with known ages. Absolute dating uses radiology and X-rays to examine the decay inside the fossil. Knowing the age of a fossil helps paleontologists understand and organize the history of our world.

The first paleontologist was a man named George Cuvier. He believed that the Earth was ancient and that catastrophes occasionally happened and wiped out a number of species. Cuvier reached this conclusion by examining fossils of mammoths and realizing they were unlike any living creature. He's considered the founding father of paleontology.

Some paleontologists think there was a type of dinosaur that could live for 300 years!

The end of a book is usually sad. I always want to keep reading, and I'm sorry the story is over, but the end of this book is a good thing because it means you're just starting your journey into science and learning.

There are so many ways to learn about different *ologies*. Museums and libraries are a great starting point, but getting out into nature with a guidebook is another spectacular way to get going. Our definitions and list of suggested readings are another way to dive in! Good luck and have fun! Studying, observing, and asking "IsThisAnOlogy?" are great ways to explore the world.

GLOSSARY

Absolute dating: Measuring the physical properties of a fossil or object using X-rays or radiocarbon. These measurements help scientists determine the age of the object in question.

Acidic: In the caseology section, acidic means sharp-tasting or having a sour flavour. The word acidic in the marine biology section means having a pH below 7.

Antibacterial: Usually refers to an antibiotic, which is an agent that kills bacteria.

Apiarist: A person who keeps bees, especially to produce honey.

Apiologist: A person who studies bees.

Apiology: The scientific study of bees, especially honeybees.

Apoidea: This is a grouping of insects that includes bees, honeybees, and wasps.

Archaeology: The scientific study of human activity through material culture. The word comes from the Latin word *archaeologia*, meaning ancient history, and the Greek word *arkhaios*, meaning ancient.

Archean: The earliest eon of geological history! This is the time period when the Earth first formed.

Arctic tern: A type of bird known for their extremely long annual migration. They are small, slender, grey and white birds.

Arthropods: A grouping of animals that includes insects and spiders. Some of the first creatures on Earth were arthropods.

Atlantic puffin: A black and white bird with an orange beak, a species of seabird in the auk family.

Avian flu: A viral respiratory disease that affects different bird species. In rare cases, it can affect human beings.

Bacteria: These are often single-celled organisms. They are usually tiny, maybe only a few millimetres in length, and were among the first life forms to appear on Earth.

Banbury Cheese: A type of cheese mentioned by Shakespeare! This cheese is made in Banbury, England.

Binoculars: Special glasses that make faraway objects seem close. They have two refracting telescopes mounted side by side, which are aligned to point in the same direction.

Bird blind: A structure that lets you watch birds without being seen.

Birding: The identification and observation of wild birds in their natural habitat.

Cambrian explosion: This is when many animals first appeared in the fossil record. It happened 541 million years ago. Before that, most life forms were simple bacteria and single-celled organisms.

Caseology: This word is not formally recognized but is used in food and wine industries to mean the study of cheese and cheesemaking. It's a delicious *ology*!

Cenozoic: This era began about 65 million years ago and continues to the present. Most of the animals we know today start showing up in the time period, including humans.

Cephalopod: Any member of the mollusc class of animals and includes squids, octopus, and cuttlefish. These creatures usually have a prominent head and a set of arms or tentacles.

Cheddar: Made from cow's milk, this is the most popular and widely purchased cheese on the planet. It has a hard texture and originally came from England.

Cheesemaking: The craft of making cheese.

Cleanupologist: This a made-up word! To me, it refers to someone who is interested in understanding and studying why people litter and refers to someone who is interested in cleaning our oceans and beaches. It's a very important job!

Continental drift: The theory that the continents shifted position on the Earth's surface and drifted away from each other due to plate tectonics. This idea was proposed in 1912 by geophysicist Alfred Wegener. Like many theories, it was scoffed at and rejected, only to be accepted later. Proposing a new idea requires imagination and a certain kind of bravery!

Coprolites: Fossilized poop.

Coral reefs: An underwater ecosystem composed of colonies of coral polyps stacked atop each other and connected by calcium carbonate. Coral reefs can be wondrous, colourful places.

Fossil record: This means the history of life according to or documented by the imprints of organisms from earlier geological periods.

Geology: From the Greek word *geo*, which means Earth, and the Greek suffix *-logia*, which means *the study of*, this science deals with the physical history of the Earth, rocks, minerals, and the physical and chemical changes that the Earth has undergone.

Granite: Light-coloured igneous rock with speckles that are easy to spot.

Igneous rocks: Rocks formed through the cooling of lava and magma.

K-Pg event: The famous mass extinction event that killed the dinosaurs and most animal and plant species at the end of the Cretaceous period.

Marine biology: The study of life in the oceans. The word comes from the French word *marin*, which means *of the sea*, and the Greek word *bios*, which means life.

Mesozoic: The age of the dinosaurs!

Metamorphic rocks: These form when rocks are subjected to high heat; high pressure; hot, mineral-rich fluids; or a combination of factors.

Migration: To move from one area to another. Bird migration usually refers to regular seasonal movement, either to breeding or feeding grounds.

Minerals: These are elements found in the Earth and in our bodies that we need to develop and function normally.

Mozzarella: A stretchy, white cheese created in southern Italy. It was traditionally made from water buffalo milk and it melts well.

Nectar: A sugar-rich liquid produced by plants. Bees love it!

Ology: A scientific field or field or study.

Ologist: Someone who is an expert in a specific field of study or science.

Ornithologist: A person who studies bird behaviour, physiology, and conservation of birds and bird habitats.

Ornithology: The scientific study of birds and bird behaviour. The word comes from the late sixteenth-century Latin word *ornithologia*, meaning bird science.

Paleozoic: This era was full of dramatic climate, geological, and evolutionary change! The Cambrian explosion happened during this period.

Pollination: The process of transferring pollen from the male anther of a flower to a female stigma of another flower. Pollination is very important so that more plants can grow!

Precambrian: One of the earliest geological ages. Paleontologists and geologists can tell if something is *Precambrian* by examining different layers of sedimentary rock.

Relative dating: The process of determining if one rock or fossil is older or younger by comparing that rock to other specimens.

Sedimentary rocks: Formed from pre-existing rocks or pieces of dead organisms. Sedimentary rocks often have distinctive layering or bedding.

RECOMMENDED READING

If you're interested in birds, bird behaviour, or ornithologists, then the following books might be helpful:

The Big Book of Birds by Yuval Zommer

Nests by Susan Ogilvy

The Lost Words by Robert Macfarlane

The Boy Who Drew Birds: A Story of John James Audubon by Jacqueline Davies

Birds of Newfoundland: Field Guide by Ian Warkentin and Sandy Newton

If you're interested in cheesemaking, flavour, and cooking, then check out these titles and this video series!

Say Cheese!: A Kid's Guide to Cheese Making with Recipes for Mozzarella, Cream Cheese, Feta, and Other Favorites by Ricki Carroll and Sarah Carroll

Transformed: How Everyday Things Are Made by Bill Slavin

A Brie(f) History of Cheese by Paul Kindstedt: Available through TED-Ed: https://www.youtube.com/watch?v=QKae1k1BDdA&ab_channel=TED-Ed

If geology excites you, then you might enjoy reading about rocks, minerals, and the first geologists!

The Street Beneath My Feet by Charlotte Guillain and Yuval Zommer

Grand Canyon by Jason Chin

Super Earth Encyclopedia by DK, with contributions by Smithsonian Institution

National Geographic Kids Geology 101 https://kids.nationalgeographic.com/science/article/geology-101

If it's marine biology or cleanupology that's captured your attention, try:

The Ocean in Your Bathtub by Seth Fishman

We Are Water Protectors by Carole Lindstrom

The Mess That We Made by Michelle Lord

Old Enough to Save the Planet by Loll Kirby

When the Whales Walked: And Other Incredible Evolutionary Journeys by Dougal Dixon

Our Planet: The One Place We All Call Home by Matt Whyman

Bees are pretty cool! If you're interested in learning more, check out these titles:

Daphne's Bees by Catherine Dempsey

Bees: A Honeyed History by Piotr Socha

Pollen: Darwin's 130-Year Prediction by Darcy Pattison

Finally, here are some ways to learn more about dinosaurs, fossils, and paleontology:

Dinosaurs Bones: And What They Tell Us by Rob Colson

When Sue Found Sue: Sue Hendrickson Discovers Her T. Rex by Toni Buzzeo

Dinosaur Lady: The Daring Discoveries of Mary Anning by Linda Skeers

Out of the Blue: How Animals Evolved from Prehistoric Seas by Elizabeth Shreeve